92
SPI

Olsen, James T.

Mark Spitz: the
shark

DATE			

MARK. SPITZ
THE SHARK

By James T. Olsen

Illustrated by Harold Henriksen

Text copyright © 1974 by Educreative Systems, Inc. Illustrations copyright © 1974 by Creative Education. International copyrights reserved in all countries. No part of this book may be reproduced in any form without written permission from the publisher. Printed in the United States.

Library of Congress Number: 73-11018   ISBN: O-87191-263-5

Published by Creative Education, Mankato, Minnesota 56001
Prepared for the Publisher by Educreative Systems, Inc.
Distributed by Childrens Press, 1224 West Van Buren Street, Chicago, Illinois 60607

Library of Congress Cataloging in Publication Data
  James T. Olsen
  Mark Spitz: Mark the shark.
  SUMMARY: Biography of the swimmer who won seven gold medals in the 1972 Olympics.
  1. Spitz, Mark—Juvenile literature. [1. Spitz, Mark. 2. Swimming—Biography]
I. Title. GV838.S68E38 797.2'1'0924 [B] [92] 73-11018 ISBN 0-87191-264-3

4

Lights. Cheering people. Flashing white teeth below a dark mustache. The flash of gold. Lots of gold. Seven gold medals to be exact. The teeth, the mustache and the medals all belong to a young swimmer. "Mark the Shark" screamed the crowd. It was the top of the world—and the end of the line for Mark Andrew Spitz, the man who won seven gold medals for his swimming in the 1972 Olympics.

Mark Spitz practiced swimming every single day of his life. During the school year, he would swim for three hours every day. When school would let out for the summer, Mark would swim four hours every day. Imagine jumping into a pool, the water's chilly. You start to swim. Back and forth. Several hundred times! You are working so hard that your body gives off a lot of steam. Your chest hurts. It gets harder and harder to breathe. The muscles in your upper arms and thighs are so sore they feel as though they are on fire. You are finally finished for the day. But you'll be at it again tomorrow!

The Shark really did swim to get to the top. And swam and swam some more. Mark has been a water baby since he was two years old. His mother remembers the first time he saw the ocean: "You should have seen that little boy dash into the ocean. He'd run like he was trying to commit suicide."

When Mark was eight years old his father, Arnold Spitz, signed him up for a swimming program at the Y.M.C.A. At 9 his father turned him over to Sherm Chavoor, a man who has coached many Olympic swimmers. He worked out for an hour or more every Monday, Wednesday and Friday and for twice as long on Saturdays. At ten he added a half hour of practice to each day. By the time he was ten years old, Spitz held seventeen national age group swimming records and set his first U.S. swim record.

As a child Mark learned the importance of winning, at least as far as his parents were concerned.

Mark was Jewish and it was expected that he go to Hebrew classes after school. There weren't enough hours in Mark's day for school, swimming and Hebrew classes. Mr. Spitz went to talk to the Hebrew teacher. "Rabbi, even God likes a winner," he said. That was the end of the Hebrew lessons.

When Mark was swimming his father was often with him.

"Mark, how many lanes in the pool?" he would ask.

"Six," Mark would answer.

"And how many lanes win?"

"One, only one," was what Mark would say.

The years went on and Mark didn't seem to get better fast enough. When he was fourteen years old, Mark's father talked to him, "We have to do something now—or nothing . . . you can forget about competitive swimming. Or we can go to Santa Clara and turn you over to George Haines." George Haines is the coach of the famous Santa Clara Swim Club and was the coach of the 1968 United States Olympic Swimming Team. Mark chose to go to Santa Clara and study with Haines. The family moved and Mark's father quit the job he'd had for 18 years.

A lot of the Spitz family life revolved around Mark's swimming and Mark worked very hard. It wasn't only hard work or the way his family felt that made Mark good, though. His body was built for swimming. From his wide shoulders hang a pair of long arms that end with giant cup-like hands. Those hands can scoop through the water like giant steam shovels lifting dirt and rock. The World's No. 1 swimmer is also able to bend his legs forward at the knee, not only backwards. That means that he can kick anywhere from six to twelve inches deeper than any other swimmer. In addition, he has a very long stroke. He can swim the length of a seventy-five foot swimming pool with only thirteen strokes. Most swimmers take anywhere from fifteen to sixteen strokes.

9

When Coach Haines looked Mark over he was impressed by his knees! "He'll probably be the best swimmer in the world," he said. Mark puts it well when he says, "I'm slower but I'm faster. I mean that I stroke slower—but I get there faster." He was right. By the time he was 18 he was already known as one of the world's great swimmers. Over the next two years, Spitz won 22 national and international titles. He shattered ten world records. Of course, he is the current world record holder in both the hundred meter butterfly (55.7 seconds) and the 200 meter butterfly (2 minutes, 5.7 seconds).

There were problems though. At one point Mark wasn't allowed to swim in the N.C.A.A. meet. A lot of people felt this was done so he wouldn't embarrass the older swimmers by beating them.

Mark studied with Haines and he learned many things. When Spitz came up against Don Scholander those years of learning and hard work really showed. Scholander was Spitz's rival. They swam together a lot and Don was Mark's hero. Mark wanted to top the older boy's total of four gold medals at the 1964 Olympics. Don really didn't care very much for Spitz. It must have been hard for him to know that Mark might end up a better swimmer than he was. Mark tried to outswim Don, even at daily practice. Scho-

lander's feeling showed when he said, "Mark is not very smart. Mark is interested in his gold medal counting."

Mark, and other people in his life as it turned out, were interested in that kind of counting and he took Scholander's place at the top. At twenty-two years of age, Scholander's big swimming days were almost over. The two swimmers faced one another at the Long Beach swimming pool. It was in this pool that Spitz and Scholander fought it out in the 100 meter free style.

The Star Spangled Banner was played. Three blond girls in yellow swimsuits floated the length of the pool on their backs. They carried U.S. flags across their chests and were careful not to let those flags get wet. As soon as the girls got out of the pool, the gun sounded. The race between the two men was on. Scholander lost. Spitz later told newsmen that he was disappointed. He didn't feel that Don tried hard enough to beat him. He was also disappointed in himself. He had counted on winning in less time. Scholander had a very simple feeling about the whole thing. "Swimming is like cowboys and Indians. Sooner or later you outgrow it." Mark didn't agree at all.

The winning was great, but Mark found a part of his swimming life very hard. Like anyone else Mark wanted friends. Many of the other swimmers didn't like him. They kept putting him down and it was hard on him. Coach Sherm Chavoor said, "He was set apart because he was so good. And he just wanted to be

one of the guys."

Mark started worrying about his health. He had earaches and sore muscles. Always a new pain. Instead of making the other swimmers feel sorry for him they only put him down harder.

In 1968, Mark was off to the Olympics in Mexico City. He was boasting that he would be the first Olympic athlete to win six gold medals. He would prove to everyone, his parents, his coaches, his fellow swimmers that the work and sacrifices were worth it. Many people thought he was a fresh kid and didn't like him talking so big. There was such bad feeling that some of his teammates cheered as they watched Mark on closed circuit T.V. They felt he got put in his place as he lost the first race. He was very disappointed because he won only two gold medals in Mexico and those were in the relay events. He won them with his team, not on his own. He also won a silver and bronze medal.

He was very unhappy. But he decided that this was not as important as the next Olympics. They were to be held in Munich, Germany in 1972.

It was not a good time in Mark's life. After he got back from Mexico he had a falling out with his coach. He refused to swim in an A.A.U. meet. He said he was tired. He also felt that Haines worried more about points for the Santa Clara swimming team than he did

about Mark. If Mark were in too many races he might be too tired to do well. If he lost he could look foolish. It would be Mexico all over again.

The team lost the meet and Haines was angry. He kicked Mark and his sister Nancy off the team. Mark was ready for a change. He said he had "outgrown being treated like a baby."

Mark went to Indiana University and a new coach, James "Doc" Counsilman. Doc was happy Spitz was there. He was good for Mark. He made Mark study hard as well as swim hard. Mark's grades got better. Doc told his other swimmers, "Mark Spitz is coming to school . . . I like him and I want you to give him a chance." They did. And the more they gave Mark a chance, the more comfortable he felt and the easier to get along with he became. He also outgrew acting like such a spoiled brat.

His relationship to his family changed too. One summer day he went to watch his sister swim. He got into a fight with his father. He felt Arnold Spitz shouldn't always have so much say about Nancy's swimming. He began to feel good about himself. He was ready to go on setting new swimming records. He was ready!

In 1972 Mark found himself in Munich, Germany in the company of 11,999 athletes from 124 different countries. Mark felt good. He had broken 28

freestyle and butterfly records. His swimming team was young and green but Mark felt very sure of winning as he watched the other teams parade by the grandstand. The Olympic flame or torch had been carried 3,500 miles by more than 5,976 runners. It now was finally in the hands of a West German runner. 80,000 enthusi-

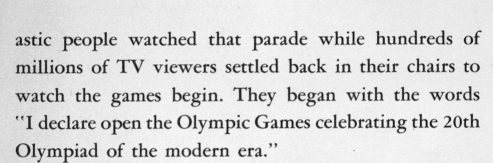

astic people watched that parade while hundreds of millions of TV viewers settled back in their chairs to watch the games begin. They began with the words "I declare open the Olympic Games celebrating the 20th Olympiad of the modern era."

And so it started. And Mark Spitz started on the last lap of his lifetime goal. First, Spitz and his teammates plowed through the water like speed boats to win the 200 meter butterfly. Spitz was a little scared. "I remembered what happened in Mexico City," he said. He may have remembered but all that was changed now as Mark knocked 2.6 seconds off his own world record. And he won the first of his 1972 gold medals. His teammates had done well, too. Gary Hall, Spitz's teammate at Indiana University, took second place. Robin Backhaus of Redlands, California took third place.

All of the Americans in Munich were very happy.

As the team coach said: "If Mark had lost his first race, he would have been discouraged. But the Mark Spitz of '72 is a tough person." There was no question. Mark was tough. Very tough. In the 400 meter freestyle relay held later that night, he took another gold medal and broke another world record. His first day of Olympian work had turned out very well. There were two gold medals around Mark's neck.

The next night he swam in the finals of the 200 meter freestyle. His teamate, Steve Genter of Lakewood, California, gave Mark his greatest competition. Genter had just been released from the hospital. There he had chest surgery for a partially collapsed lung. In spite of this, Genter decided to swim anyway and led Spitz at both the 100 and 150 meter turns. But Spitz sliced through the water at the last 50 meters and surged ahead of Genter to clip .72 second from his own world record and to win his third gold medal.

But Spitz was not finished. Not yet anyway. Two

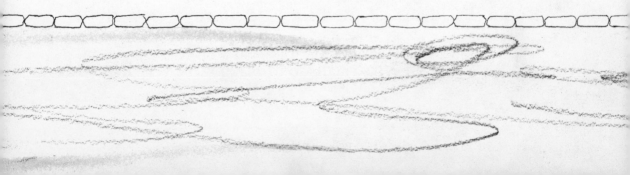

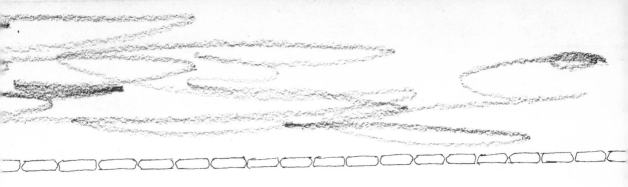

days later, Spitz was swimming once again and this time he splashed his way to more gold and more records in the 100 meter butterfly where he clocked 54.27 seconds. He also took the 800 meter freestyle relay. At that point, he had tied the record for gold medals (five) set in 1920 by an Italian fencer, Nedo Nadi. Nothing could stop Spitz now and he and the crowd and his teammates knew it. By the end of the week, he picked up Medals 6 and 7 in the 100 meter freestyle and in the 400 meter medley relay.

His teammates were right in there with him. And the crowds were with him. It looked as if he had won more than medals. Everyone was cheering "Mark the Shark." This had not always been the case. When he had first arrived at the Olympics, a passerby had said to Spitz: "Hey, Jew boy, you aren't going to win any gold medals." It may be that kind of pressure had helped Spitz. He had learned how to put it to work for him, to make him swim much more and much better.

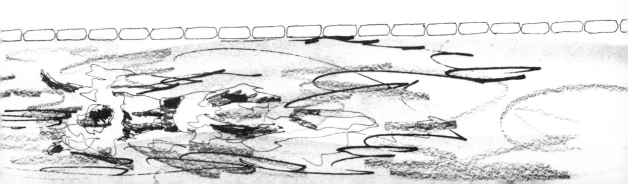

He didn't get upset and do badly. He had not always been that confident. Instead he felt sure of his ability and worked hard to win. As he himself had said one time, "I sometimes just go through the motions at workouts, but that's usually because I want the coach to baby me that day or something." Moreover, his sureness about himself showed. The days when he asked one of his coaches, "Was it clearcut that I won?" after a big race, were over.

It was certain that he had won at Munich. He was the best, the very best swimmer in the world. To prove the point, seven gold medals dangled from Mark's neck. The world record times had flashed on the scoreboard. Fan mail and requests for personal appearances piled up in his small room in the Olympic Village. When he left his room now, autograph seekers would be right behind him begging him for his autograph. Postcards with his picture on them had already sold out. Mark and his mustache were all over the place. Many people thought he looked like a movie star, Omar Sharif. The mustache helped. People teased Mark about that mustache.

Swimmers have always been very concerned about slipping through the water—quickly. Many swimmers have shaved their hair so that they would be smooth all over. That would help they thought. Not Mark. He had long, thick, dark hair and a great bushy mustache. He said it helped him swim better. It kept the water out of his mouth. It showed he felt sure enough of himself to be a little different.

All kinds of people hung around him, especially girls. For example, a French newspaper reported that he and Sandy Neilson, a surprise winner in the 100 freestyle, were in love. But then the newspapers reported that Spitz couldn't be in love with her because Spitz's true sweetheart was Jo Harshbarger, the U.S. distance swimmer. Spitz pointed out that since Harshbarger was only fifteen years of age, they were only spending some time together. After the twenty-two-year-old Spitz received his gold medal for the 200 butterfly victory, Spitz placed his medal, in a ceremony of his own, around the neck of Harshbarger with the words, "Jo's the best looking swimmer since Donna de Varona." Then he added, "I was too young for Donna and I'm too old for Jo." Jo was very happy and told the waiting newsmen that Mark was just trying to make her feel good so she could win the race. Maybe Mark remembered those cheers as he lost in Mexico.

CONCORD OXBOW SCHOOL

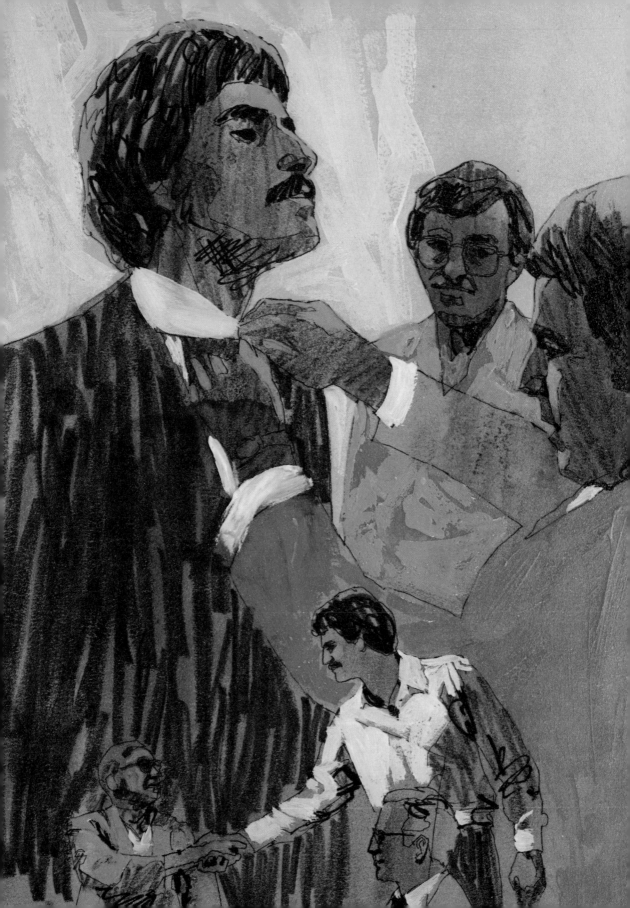

But Jo didn't win. Keena Rothhammer of the United States took that particular race. Nevertheless, because of Spitz, the United States' place as number one in Olympic Swimming was "in the bag." There was no one better than Spitz in the world and there was no country that had taken more medals in Olympic Swimming than the United States. His father and mother, his coaches—all of them had been correct in believing that one day Mark Spitz would be the Champion Swimmer of the World. Where would Mark go from here?

His plans were rather simple. He had decided that he wanted to become a dentist. As he himself had put it at one time, "I wonder how it will be when I'm Mark Spitz, just one of a million dentists, after all the travel and attention I've had as a kid." It was a good question.

Mark was very handsome with perfect white teeth, a dashing mustache and dark black hair. After his last Olympic race, Spitz still said that he was going to stop swimming and go ahead with his plan to study to be a dentist. His life had been one of practice. His whole life had been swimming. Now he was a kind of national hero. Even his room at the Olympic Village was strewn with flowers. There were flowers all over, even on his floor. People chased after him.

A change in plans for Mark Spitz has taken place. When asked about those changes in his plans, Mark Spitz simply says, "I decided to wait before continuing my education. I chose dentistry because there was nothing to swimming financially so that I needed to do something else. Swimming is a very demanding type sport; if I spent the three and a half to four and a half hours necessary every day to keep in training, I would not have been able to devote the proper amount of time to dental school to do well at it. I was in college, and I graduated, as it happened, the summer before the Olympics, so that regardless of how I did in the Olympics, whether I won the seven gold medals or lost, I knew I was going to retire from swimming. As it was, I won, and it was a good note to go out on."

What does Mark look forward to now? "I had prepared myself that this was going to be a time of change, but I wasn't prepared for this. No one told me if you practice swimming this is going to happen to you, like they might say to someone if you practice football you could be like Joe Namath. Someone wouldn't say to a child, if you practice football, you could be like Mark Spitz. Being Mark Spitz and winning seven gold medals in the Olympics doesn't necessarily mean that someone would be offered the same opportunities that I have been fortunate enough to have."

He told people how he'd felt about the past. Especially his time at Indiana University. "I'm a firm believer that you can't get good unless you train with the best. And I had the best. I think as teammates—Gary Hall, one of the outstanding swimmers of our time—we had a love for each other. The sincerity and respect we had for each other—and for the University—it's all because of Doc."

Mark is used to having other people make his decisions for him. In a remarkable interview in Sports' Illustrated, Mark's father had this to say about himself and his family: "The greatest motivating factor in Mark's life had been Lenore (Mark's mother) and myself. Because of what I have given of myself, this is what *I* created. He's a gorgeous human being; he's a beautiful person. You think this just happens? I've got my life tied up in this kid. There is nothing wrong with parents giving to their children. There was a point when I pushed him, I guess, but if I hadn't pushed my son, he would never have been at Santa Clara . . . Swimming isn't everything; winning is. Who plays to lose? I'm not out to lose. I never said to him, 'You're second; that's great.' I told him I didn't care about winning age groups; I care for world records." The new world records have been set by Mark. What's next?

Arnold Spitz, Sherm Chevoor, George Haines, Doc Counsilman. Mark has alway had an older man to tell him what to do.

He hopes to change these next years of his life. He now has an agent, Norman Brokaw. It's hard to get to talk to Mark or see him unless you see his agent first. And the new work has started, TV shows, advertising magazines and newspaper articles.

In the meantime, Mark has married a girl by the name of Susan Weiner, a twenty-year-old model who goes to U.C.L.A. She is the daughter of one of Mark's father's business friends. The couple met through their fathers. When the engaged couple were interviewed by a newspaper, they were asked what their plans for the future are. It turns out that the biggest dream the couple has is to live in a big house facing the Pacific Ocean in California. When they were asked if their house would contain a swimming pool, Mark replied with his usual calm directness, "No, this time I want my own ocean."

Only time will tell whether Mark Spitz will have his own ocean or how his life will go. It's clear the end of his swimming life is over. He has said that the most exciting moment in his whole life was hearing the Star Spangled Banner played as he stood with his seven gold medals around his neck. The top of the world but the end of the line. One line at least. What new line Mark's life will follow is a big question. What would you guess? Movie star? Swimming coach? Dentist? Maybe even the father of a second Mark the Shark?

JACK NICKLAUS
BILL RUSSELL
MARK SPITZ
VINCE LOMBARDI
BILLIE JEAN KING
ROBERTO CLEMENTE
JOE NAMATH
BOBBY HULL
HANK AARON
JERRY WEST
TOM SEAVER
JACKIE ROBINSON
MUHAMMAD ALI
O. J. SIMPSON
JOHNNY BENCH
WILT CHAMBERLAIN
ARNOLD PALMER
A. J. FOYT
JOHNNY UNITAS
GORDIE HOWE

superstars! superstars! superstars! superstars!

CREATIVE EDUCATION SPORTS SUPERSTARS

WALT FRAZIER
PHIL AND TONY ESPOSITO
BOB GRIESE
FRANK ROBINSON
PANCHO GONZALES
LEE TREVINO
KAREEM ABDUL JABBAR
JEAN CLAUDE KILLY
EVONNE GOOLAGONG
ARTHUR ASHE
SECRETARIAT
ROGER STAUBACK
FRAN TARKENTON
BOBBY ORR
LARRY CSONKA
BILL WALTON
ALAN PAGE
PEGGY FLEMING
OLGA KORBUT
DON SCHULA
MICKEY MANTLE